The Complete Chanukah Songbook

Editors
J. Mark Dunn & Joel N. Eglash

Project Manager & Typesetter
Eric S. Komar

Transcontinental Music Publications

More music, study resources and children's books for Chanukah may be found at

www.TranscontinentalMusic.com

www.URJPress.com

Hebrew Pronunciation Guide

<u>VOWELS</u>
a as in *father*
ai as in *aisle* (= long *i* as in *ice*)
e = short *e* as in *bed*
ei as in *eight* (= long *a* as in *ace*)
i as in *pizza* (= long *e* as in *be*)
o = long *o* as in *go*
u = long *u* as in *lunar*

' = unstressed vowel close to ə or unstressed short *e*
oi as in *boy*

<u>CONSONANTS</u>
ch as in German *Bach* or Scottish *loch* (not as in *cheese*)
g = hard *g* as in *get* (not soft *g* as in *gem*)
tz = as in *boats*
h after a vowel is silent

Yiddish Pronunciation Guide

<u>VOWELS</u>
a as in *father*
ai as in *aisle* (= long *i* as in *ice*)
e = short *e* as in *bed*
ei as in *eight* (= long *a* as in *ace*)
i as in *pizza* (= long *e* as in *be*)
o = long *o* as in *go*
' = unstressed vowel close to ə or unstressed short *e*

u (between consonants) = *u* as in *put*
u (at end of word) = long *u* as in *lunar*

<u>CONSONANTS</u>
ch (kh) as in German *Bach* or Scottish *loch*
(not as in *cheese*)
g = hard *g* as in *get* (not soft *g* as in *gem*)
tz = as in *boats*

Ladino Pronunciation Guide

D	Pronounced like "th"	as in *this*	*C*	Pronounced like unvoiced S	as in *sorry*
G	Before e or i, like "dj"	as in *gentle*	*Z*	Voiced S sound	as in *lazy*
J	Not gutturalized	as in *vision*	*X*	Pronounced like "sh"	as in *shoe*
LL	Pronounced as "y"	as in *yet*	*V*	As "v" in English	as in *victory*
S	When initial - unvoiced	as in *sorry*		(not mixture of b and v)	
	When between vowels - voiced	as in *lazy*			
	When final - voiced	as in *lazy*		*Vowels pronounced same as Hebrew*	

No part of this book may be reproduced in any manner without written permission from the publisher.
No sound recording featuring the works in this book may be made
without proper mechanical license from an authorized licensing authority.

THE COMPLETE CHANUKAH SONGBOOK

© 2003 Transcontinental Music Publications
A division of the Union for Reform Judaism
633 Third Avenue - New York, NY 10017 - Fax 212.650.4119
212.650.4101 - www.TranscontinentalMusic.com - tmp@urj.org

Manufactured in the United States of America
Cover art © Michele Pulver Feldman
Cover design by Pine Point Productions, Windham, ME • Book design by Joel N. Eglash
ISBN 8074-0910-3
10 9 8 7 6 5 4 3 2

UNION FOR
REFORM JUDAISM
תאחוד לתחדות רפורמית
SERVING REFORM CONGREGATIONS IN NORTH AMERICA

DISTRIBUTED BY

HAL•LEONARD®

7777 W. BLUEMOUND RD. P.O. BOX 13819 MILWAUKEE, WI 53213

TABLE OF CONTENTS

PREFACE

What does Chanukah mean?
The Hebrew word *Chanukah* (Hanukkah, Hanukah) means "dedication" and refers to the joyous eight-day celebration through which Jews commemorate the victory of the Maccabees over the armies of Syria in 165 B.C.E. and the subsequent liberation and "rededication" of the Temple in Jerusalem.

Is Chanukah biblically based?
Unlike most Jewish holidays, Chanukah is not mentioned in the *Torah* (Five Books of Moses), Prophets, or Writings. The historical events upon which the celebration is based are recorded in I and II Maccabees, two books contained within a later collection of writings known as the Apocrypha.

How did Chanukah become so popular?
Technically, Chanukah is considered a "minor" Jewish festival. Yet it ranks along with *Pesach* (Passover) and *Purim* as one of the most beloved Jewish family holidays. Clearly, the stirring story associated with Chanukah, the rituals that emerged from it, and the special Chanukah games and foods combined to capture the imagination and elevate its status within the Jewish community.

An Introduction to Chanukah

What is the story of Chanukah?

In the year 168 B.C.E., the Syrian tyrant Antiochus Epiphanes sent his soldiers to Jerusalem. The Syrians desecrated the Temple, and Antiochus abolished Judaism. The only options he offered Jews were conversion or death. Altars and idols were set up throughout Judea for the purpose of worshiping Greek gods. Antiochus outlawed the observance of the Sabbath, the Festivals, and circumcision.

In the Hebrew month of *Kislev* (around December), the Temple was desecrated by Antiochus and the Jews were forced commit idolatry. Thousands chose to die instead. Among these martyrs was a woman named Hannah who, with her seven sons, defied the Syrian decree.

Slowly, a resistance movement developed against the cruelty of Antiochus, led by a priestly family known as the Hasmoneans, or Maccabees. The head of the family was an elderly man named Mattathias. He and his five sons left Jerusalem and took up residence in a small town north of Jerusalem, called Modi'in. When Syrian soldiers appeared in the town and commanded the inhabitants to offer sacrifices to Zeus, Mattathias and his sons refused. Mattathias killed one Jew who began to sacrifice to Zeus, and his sons then turned upon the Syrian troops and slew them.

It was a turning point in the struggle. The Maccabees became instant folk heroes. Fleeing to the hills with their followers, they conducted a campaign of guerilla warfare against the occupying Syrian forces. Mattathias's son, Judah, known as "the Hammer," became the chief strategist and military leader.

Furious, Antiochus decided to destroy the people of Judea. He sent a large army, with instructions to kill every man, woman, and child. Though outnumbered, Judah Maccabee and his fighters miraculously won two major battles, routing the Syrians decisively. By 165 B.C.E., the terror of Antiochus had ended. The Jews had won a victory for their land and their faith.

The idols were torn down, and, on the morning of the twenty-fifth day of *Kislev* in 165 B.C.E., the Temple in Jerusalem was reconsecrated—three years to the day after its original defilement. In celebration, the people of Jerusalem lit bright lights in front of their homes and decided to mark their deliverance with an annual eight-day festival. It was called the Feast of Lights, the Feast of Dedication, or simply Chanukah.

Jews continue the ancient customs related to Chanukah today, commemorating the liberation of the Jewish people and their affirmation of human dignity and freedom of religion. In Jewish homes throughout the world, the eve of the twenty-fifth day of *Kislev* begins an eight-day celebration involving many joyous customs and ceremonies. The modern home celebration of Chanukah centers around the lighting of Chanukah candles in the menorah, unique foods, and special games and songs.

Songs of the Chanukah Story

LIGHTS

Why do Jews celebrate Chanukah for eight days? What about the jar of oil that burned for eight days?

Originally, the eight-day Feast of Lights was intended to parallel the eight days of the Fall harvest festival, *Sukkot*. The story of the Maccabees made no mention of the beautiful legend concerning the jar of oil that has come to be a part of Chanukah. Several centuries later (500 C.E.), the story of the cruse of oil emerged in the *Talmud* (book from approximately 200 C.E. of Jewish religious legal and ethical teachings).

The legend relates that when the Maccabees entered the Temple and began to cleanse it, they immediately relit the *neir tamid*, or "eternal light." A single jar of oil remained, which was sufficient for only one day. The messenger who was sent to secure additional oil took eight days to complete his mission. But, miraculously, the single cruse of oil continued to burn for eight days. The Rabbis of the Talmud, therefore, attributed the eight days of Chanukah to the miracle of the little jar of oil.

What is the meaning of menorah?

Menorah is a Hebrew word meaning "candelabrum." In relation to Chanukah, it refers to the nine-branched ceremonial lamp in which the Chanukah candles are placed and then blessed.

Is the menorah unique to Chanukah?

No. The menorah originated as a religious symbol in biblical times. The Torah records how the great artist Bezalel fashioned a seven-branched menorah for the desert Tabernacle. Such a seven-branched menorah adorned the Temple in Jerusalem and was carried away by the Roman legions at the time of its destruction in 70 C.E.

How did the Chanukah menorah originate?

The nine-branched Chanukah menorah, also called a *chanukiyah*, was a modification of the biblical model and seems to have originated in the first century C.E. It had eight branches, one for each day of the holiday, and a ninth branch for the *shamash* or "servant" light.

In ancient times, oil was used in the menorah. Over time, candles were substituted for the oil. Some scholars believe that the use of small candles for the menorah was a deliberate choice, designed to distinguish Chanukah lights from Christian votive candles. Except in times of religious persecution, the menorah was placed outside the front door or, as is the custom today, displayed in the window of every Jewish home.

How does one light the Chanukah candles?

In a celebrated talmudic dispute, two Jewish teachers, Hillel and Shammai, argued whether one should begin by lighting eight candles and gradually decrease to one (Shammai), or begin with one candle and add an additional one each night, thus continuously increasing the light and joy of the holiday (Hillel). The majority ruled with Hillel. Thus, on the first night of Chanukah, Jews recite or chant the blessings and light one candle with the shamash, two on the second night, and so on. Customarily, the candles are placed in the menorah from right to left but lit from left to right.

SONGS OF LIGHT

LITURGY

What are the Chanukah candle blessings?

There are two blessings that are chanted or recited on every night of Chanukah. The first is a blessing over the candles themselves: *Baruch Atah Adonai, Eloheinu Melech ha-olam, asher kid'shanu b'mitzvotav v'tzivanu l'hadlik ner shel Chanukah.* "Blessed are You, Adonai our God, Ruler of the world, who has sanctified us by Your commandments and commanded us to kindle the Chanukah lights."

The second blessing expresses thanks for the "miracle" of deliverance: *Baruch Atah Adonai, Eloheinu Melech ha-olam, she-asah nisim la-avoteinu bayamim haheim baz'man hazeh.* "Blessed are You, Adonai our God, Ruler of the world, who did wondrous things for our ancestors in former times at this season."

There is a third blessing that is chanted or recited only on the first night. This is the *Shehecheyanu* prayer, pronounced by Jews on happy occasions: *Baruch Atah Adonai, Eloheinu Melech ha-olam, shehecheyanu v'kiy'manu v'higianu laz'man hazeh.* "Blessed are You, Adonai our God, Ruler of the world, who has kept us in life, sustained us, and brought us to this happy time."

Any member or members of the family may chant or recite the blessings. One person lights and holds the *shamash*, the blessings are pronounced, and the candles are then lit. On the Sabbath, the Chanukah candles are lit before Sabbath candles.

SONGS FROM THE LITURGY

THE DREIDL

How did the game of *dreidl* come to be associated with Chanukah?

Dreidl is a derivative of a German word meaning "top," and the game is an adaptation of an old German gambling game. Chanukah was one of the few times of the year when the rabbis permitted games of chance. The dreidl, therefore, was a natural candidate for Chanukah entertainment. The four sides of the top bear four Hebrew letters: *nun*, *gimel*, *hei*, and *shin*. Players would begin by "anteing" a certain number of coins, nuts, or other objects. Each one in turn would then spin the dreidl and proceed as follows: *nun* ("nichts")—take nothing; *gimel* ("ganz")—take everything; *hei* ("halb")—take half; *shin* ("shtell")—put in.

ש ה ג נ

shin   hei   gimel   nun

The winner would often receive money (Chanukah *gelt*). Over time, the gambling terms were reinterpreted to stand for the Hebrew statement *Neis gadol hayah sham*, "A great miracle happened there." Thus, even an ordinary game of chance was invested with Jewish values and served to remind Jews of the important message of Chanukah. Today, Jewish children throughout the world continue to enjoy the game of dreidl. In Israel, one letter on the dreidl has been changed. The *shin* has been replaced with a *pei*, transforming the Hebrew statement into *Neis gadol hayah po*, "A great miracle happened here."

פ ה ג נ

pei   hei   gimel   nun

DREIDL SONGS

THE FOODS OF CHANUKAH

Why do Jews eat *latkes* (potato pancakes) on Chanukah?
A common explanation is that Jews eat latkes because they are cooked in oil and thus are a reminder of the miracle of the single cruse of oil.

Rabbi Solomon Freehof, a twentieth-century Jewish scholar, has hypothesized that the eating of latkes may have grown out of an old custom of eating dairy foods on Chanukah. Dairy foods evolved into dairy pancakes and then into latkes, possibly because the main potato crop became available about the time of Chanukah in Northern Europe. No one knows for certain how the association began, but for anyone who feasts on latkes at Chanukah time, a historical rationale is unnecessary. The Jews of Southern Europe and elsewhere eat different fried foods on Chanukah, including *sufganiyot* (jelly-filled doughnuts).

Adapted from The Jewish Home (Revised Edition) *by Daniel Syme (URJ Press, 2004)*

FOOD SONGS

The Complete
Chanukah
Songbook

Al HaNisim

Words: Chanukah liturgy, Sofrim 20:8
Music: Dov Frimer

We give thanks for the miracles, for the times You saved us, for the mighty acts, for the victories, and for the battles You waged for our ancestors in those days at this time.

עַל הַנִּסִּים וְעַל הַפֻּרְקָן
וְעַל הַגְּבוּרוֹת וְעַל הַתְּשׁוּעוֹת,
וְעַל הַמִּלְחָמוֹת שֶׁעָשִׂיתָ לַאֲבוֹתֵינוּ
בַּיָּמִים הָהֵם בַּזְּמַן הַזֶּה.

Also available for SATB choir, piano, and optional clarinet (991306).

Al HaNisim

Words: Chanukah liturgy, Sofrim 20:8
Music: Folktune

4

We give thanks for the miracles,
for the times You saved us, for the
mighty acts, and for the victories
You waged for our ancestors in
those days at this time.

In the days of the Hasmoneans, the
great priest Mattathias, son of Yochanan,
and his sons, the Greeks rose up against
our people Israel to make us forget Your
Torah and turn away from obedience to
Your will. But You, in Your great mercy,
were on their side in their time of trouble.

עַל הַנִּסִּים וְעַל הַפֻּרְקָן וְעַל הַגְּבוּרוֹת
וְעַל הַתְּשׁוּעוֹת, שֶׁעָשִׂיתָ לַאֲבוֹתֵינוּ
בַּיָּמִים הָהֵם, בַּזְּמַן הַזֶּה.

בִּימֵי מַתִּתְיָהוּ בֶּן יוֹחָנָן כֹּהֵן גָּדוֹל,
חַשְׁמוֹנָאִי וּבָנָיו, כְּשֶׁעָמְדָה מַלְכוּת
יָוָן עַל עַמְּךָ יִשְׂרָאֵל לְהַשְׁכִּיחָם
תּוֹרָתֶךָ וּלְהַעֲבִירָם מֵחֻקֵּי רְצוֹנֶךָ.
וְאַתָּה בְּרַחֲמֶיךָ הָרַבִּים עָמַדְתָּ
לָהֶם בְּעֵת צָרָתָם.

Al HaNisim

Words: Chanukah liturgy, Sofrim 20:8
Music: Jon Nelson

u - - - vaz' - man ha - zeh.

Vs 2 V' - chol ha - cha - yim yo - du - cha, se - lah,___

vi - ha - l' - lu___ etshim - cha be - e - met,___

ha - Eil___ Y' - shu - a - tei - nu___

v' - Ez - ra - tei - - nu,___ se - lah.

For all these things, Eternal God,
let Your name be forever exalted
and blessed.

We give thanks for the miracles,
for the times You saved us, for the
mighty acts, for the victories, and
for the battles You waged for our
ancestors in those days at this time.

Let all who live affirm You and
praise Your name in truth, O God,
our Redeemer and Helper.

וְעַל כֻּלָּם יִתְבָּרַךְ וְיִתְרוֹמַם שִׁמְךָ,
מַלְכֵּנוּ, תָּמִיד לְעוֹלָם וָעֶד.

עַל הַנִּסִּים וְעַל הַפֻּרְקָן
וְעַל הַגְּבוּרוֹת וְעַל הַתְּשׁוּעוֹת,
וְעַל הַמִּלְחָמוֹת שֶׁעָשִׂיתָ לַאֲבוֹתֵינוּ
בַּיָּמִים הָהֵם וּבַזְּמַן הַזֶּה.

וְכֹל הַחַיִּים יוֹדוּךָ סֶּלָה,
וִיהַלְלוּ אֶת שִׁמְךָ בֶּאֱמֶת,
הָאֵל יְשׁוּעָתֵנוּ וְעֶזְרָתֵנוּ סֶלָה.

Al HaNisim

Words: Chanukah liturgy, Sofrim 20:8
Music: Robbie Solomon

Also available for 2-part choir, keyboard, flute, clarinet (993175).

man ___ ha - zeh, baz' - - - man ___ ha - zeh.

C Give thanks for the mi - ra - cles and sac - ri - fi - ces as in

each gen - er - a - tion a he - ro a - ri - ses to save us from ty - rants who

seek our de - mise. Give thanks un - to God who has stood by our side.
(alt. lyrics: Give thanks and re - joice with our Cha - nu - kah lights.)

10

lai lai lai la lai lai lai la lai___ lai lai la lai

lai la lai lai lai la lai___ lai lai lai lai la lai

lai lai la lai lai la lai lai___ lai lai la lai lai___

Al ha - nis - sim___ v' - al ha - pur - kan, v' - al hag' - vu -

We give thanks for the miracles,
for the times You saved us, for the
mighty acts, and for the victories
You waged for our ancestors in
those days at this time.

עַל הַנִּסִּים וְעַל הַפֻּרְקָן וְעַל הַגְּבוּרוֹת
וְעַל הַתְּשׁוּעוֹת, שֶׁעָשִׂיתָ לַאֲבוֹתֵינוּ
בַּיָּמִים הָהֶם, בַּזְּמַן הַזֶּה.

Al HaNisim

Words: Chanukah liturgy, Sofrim 20:8
Music: Craig Taubman

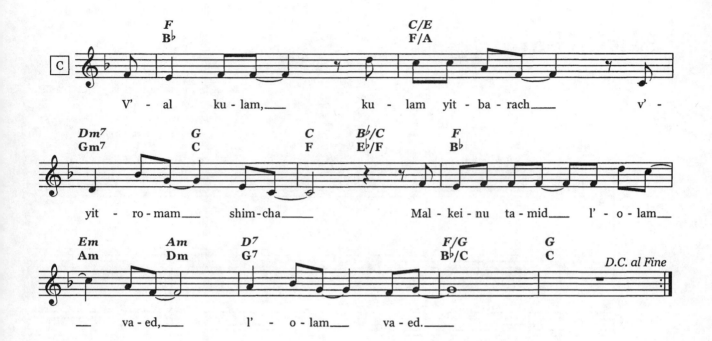

V' - al ku - lam,___ ku - lam yit - ba - rach___ v' -

yit - ro - mam___ shim - cha___ Mal - kei - nu ta - mid___ l' - o - lam___

___ va - ed,___ l' - o - lam___ va - ed.___

We give thanks for the miracles,
for the times You saved us, for the
mighty acts, for the victories, and
for the battles You waged for our
ancestors in those days at this time.

For all these things, Eternal God,
let Your name be forever exalted
and blessed.

עַל הַנִּסִּים וְעַל הַפֻּרְקָן
וְעַל הַגְּבוּרוֹת וְעַל הַתְּשׁוּעוֹת,
וְעַל הַמִּלְחָמוֹת שֶׁעָשִׂיתָ לַאֲבוֹתֵינוּ
בַּיָּמִים הָהֵם בַּזְּמַן הַזֶּה.

וְעַל כֻּלָּם יִתְבָּרַךְ וְיִתְרוֹמַם שְׁמְךָ,
מַלְכֵּנוּ, תָּמִיד לְעוֹלָם וָעֶד.

Al HaNisim

Words: Chanukah liturgy, Sofrim 20:8
Music: Max Janowski

17

dol, Chash-mo-nai u-va-nav, k'-she-a-m'-dah___ mal-chut___ Ya-

van ha-r'-sha-ah al a-m'-cha___ Yis-ra-eil,

al a-m'-cha Yis-ra-eil, l'-hash-ki-cham___

To - ra-te - cha u-l'-ha-a-vi-ram mei-chu-kei r'-tzo - ne-cha.

We give thanks for the miracles, for the times You saved us, for the mighty acts, and for the victories You waged for our ancestors in those days at this time.

In the days of the Hasmoneans, the great priest Mattathias, son of Yochanan, and his sons, the Greeks rose up against our people Israel to make us forget Your Torah and turn away from obedience to Your will. But You, in Your great mercy, were on their side in their time of trouble.

עַל הַנִּסִים וְעַל הַפֻּרְקָן וְעַל הַגְּבוּרוֹת וְעַל הַתְּשׁוּעוֹת, שֶׁעָשִׂיתָ לַאֲבוֹתֵֽינוּ בַּיָּמִים הָהֵם, בַּזְּמַן הַזֶּה.

בִּימֵי מַתִּתְיָֽהוּ בֶּן יוֹחָנָן כֹּהֵן גָּדוֹל, חַשְׁמוֹנָאִי וּבָנָיו, כְּשֶׁעָמְדָה מַלְכוּת יָוָן עַל עַמְּךָ יִשְׂרָאֵל לְהַשְׁכִּיחָם תּוֹרָתֶֽךָ וּלְהַעֲבִירָם מֵחֻקֵּי רְצוֹנֶֽךָ. וְאַתָּה בְּרַחֲמֶֽיךָ הָרַבִּים עָמַֽדְתָּ לָהֶם בְּעֵת צָרָתָם.

20

Al HaNisim

Words: Chanukah liturgy, Sofrim 20:8
Music: Michael Isaacson

24

We give thanks for the miracles,
for the times You saved us, for the
mighty acts, for the victories, and
for the battles You waged for our
ancestors in those days at this time.

[Our ancestors] dedicated these
days to give thanks and praise
Your great name.

עַל הַנִּסִּים וְעַל הַפֻּרְקָן
וְעַל הַגְּבוּרוֹת וְעַל הַתְּשׁוּעוֹת,
וְעַל הַמִּלְחָמוֹת שֶׁעָשִׂיתָ לַאֲבוֹתֵינוּ
בַּיָּמִים הָהֵם, בַּזְּמַן הַזֶּה.

וְקָבְעוּ שְׁמוֹנַת יְמֵי חֲנֻכָּה אֵלוּ
לְהוֹדוֹת וּלְהַלֵּל לְשִׁמְךָ הַגָּדוֹל.

Al HaNisim

(4-part round)

Words: Chanukah liturgy, Sofrim 20:8
Music: J. Mark Dunn

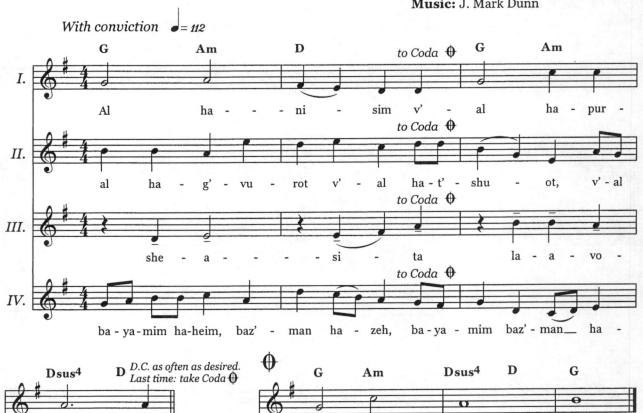

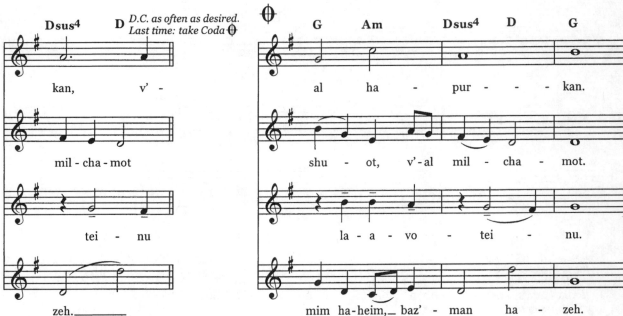

We give thanks for the miracles, for the times You saved us, for the mighty acts, and for the victories You waged for our ancestors in those days at this time.

עַל הַנִּסִּים וְעַל הַפֻּרְקָן וְעַל הַגְּבוּרוֹת
וְעַל הַתְּשׁוּעוֹת, שֶׁעָשִׂיתָ לַאֲבוֹתֵינוּ
בַּיָּמִים הָהֵם, בַּזְּמַן הַזֶּה.

Alei Neiri

Words: Indleman
Music: arr. Samuel Rosenbaum

*Burn little candle and tell of
the great miracle: of a hero
who saved our people and
rekindled the flame.*

עֲלֵי נֵרִי, עֲלֵי הַנֵּר
עַל רֹב נִסִּים, סַפֵּר, סַפֵּר.
סַפֵּר, סַפֵּר עַל אִישׁ גִּבּוֹר
הִצִּיל הָעָם, הִדְלִיק הָאוֹר.

Another Year, Another Chanukah

Jeff Klepper & Dan Freelander

28

Antiochus

Jackie Cytrynbaum

Banu Choshech L'gareish

Words: S. Levy-Tannai
Music: I. Amiran, arr. J. Mark Dunn

We came to banish the darkness,
We hold in our hands light and fire.
Each one of us is a small light,
And together a great light.
Be gone darkness and blackness,
Be gone, away from the light.

בָּאנוּ חֹשֶׁךְ לְגָרֵשׁ, בְּיָדֵנוּ אוֹר וָאֵשׁ,
כָּל אֶחָד הוּא אוֹר קָטָן, וְכֻלָּנוּ אוֹר אֵיתָן.
סוּרָה חֹשֶׁךְ הָלְאָה שְׁחוֹר,
סוּרָה מִפְּנֵי הָאוֹר.

31

Be Human

Craig Taubman, based on
Pirkei Avot 2:7

(instrumental)

Does it real - ly mat - ter? Why both - er to care?

I've heard all the rea - sons, and may - be life is - n't fair.

The right - eous will suf - fer, the wick - ed take re - ward.

Tell me, is there some sec - ret? What is good - ness for?

Yes, we can stand a - bove the crowd, raise our voic - es loud,

from our ac - tions be proud. Yes, we must rise a - bove our fears,

draw the e - ne - my near. Not by might, but by spi - rit we are here.

The more Torah, the more life.
The more study, the more wisdom.
The more counsel, the more understanding.
The more justice, the more peace.

מַרְבֶּה תוֹרָה, מַרְבֶּה חַיִּים.
מַרְבֶּה יְשִׁיבָה, מַרְבֶּה חָכְמָה.
מַרְבֶּה עֵצָה, מַרְבֶּה תְבוּנָה.
מַרְבֶּה צְדָקָה, מַרְבֶּה שָׁלוֹם.

Blessings over the Chanukah Lights

trad., arr. A.W. Binder

Blessed are You, Eternal God, Ruler of the universe, who makes us holy with Your mitzvot and commands us to kindle the lights of Chanukah.

Blessed are You, Eternal God, Ruler of the universe, who performed miracles for our ancestors in those days at this time.

Blessed are You, Eternal God, Ruler of the universe, for giving us life, for sustaining us, and for bringing us to this season.

בָּרוּךְ אַתָּה, יְיָ אֱלֹהֵינוּ, מֶלֶךְ הָעוֹלָם,
אֲשֶׁר קִדְּשָׁנוּ בְּמִצְוֹתָיו וְצִוָּנוּ
לְהַדְלִיק נֵר שֶׁל חֲנֻכָּה.

בָּרוּךְ אַתָּה, יְיָ אֱלֹהֵינוּ, מֶלֶךְ הָעוֹלָם,
שֶׁעָשָׂה נִסִּים לַאֲבוֹתֵינוּ
בַּיָּמִים הָהֵם בַּזְּמַן הַזֶּה.

בָּרוּךְ אַתָּה, יְיָ אֱלֹהֵינוּ, מֶלֶךְ הָעוֹלָם,
שֶׁהֶחֱיָנוּ וְקִיְּמָנוּ וְהִגִּיעָנוּ לַזְּמַן הַזֶּה.

Bring on the Light

Danny Maseng

Commissioned by Congregation Rodeph Shalom by
the Cantor Ephraim Biran Music Endowment Fund

May all your dreams be dreams of bright to - mor - rows.

Just light the flame; just set your sor - rows free, and

know the light___ you light___ you light___ for all___ the world___ to see.___

Bring on the light; don't fear the dark - ness.

Let ev - ery can - dle shine the light of free - dom.

Just light the flame; it's up to you and me, and

know the light___ we give___ we give___ for all___ the world___ to see.___

Vs 2 And when your heart is filled with hope, and when your

soul is filled with mu - sic, just lift your voice and sing of

joy in the night, in the night. And o-pen wide the
gates of light, and flood the__ world with love__ and__
free-dom. May ev-ery wish and ev-ery prayer be-come__ a
torch of jus-tice shin-ing ev-er bright-ly through the night.
Light the light, light the light. Each ho-ly spark, each
bles-sing that we kin-dle lights a new to-mor-row. Light the light.
Bring on the light; don't fear the dark-ness.
Let ev-ery can-dle shine the light of free-dom.
Just light the flame; it's up to you and me, and

These candles do we light in remembrance of the miracles and wonders.

הַנֵּרוֹת הַלָּלוּ אָנוּ מַדְלִיקִין
עַל הַנִּסִּים וְעַל הַנִּפְלָאוֹת.

Burn, Little Candles

Ray M. Cook

Melt, lit-tle can-dles, melt melt melt. You have been such fun.

Eight lit-tle can-dles go to sleep, when the day is done.

42

Chanukah (Chag Yafeh)

Words: L. Kipnis
Music: Folktune

Joyfully ♩ = 120

Cha - nu - kah, Cha - nu - kah, chag ya - feh kol kach.
Cha - nu - kah, Cha - nu - kah, ein cha - lon b'li eish.

Or cha - viv mi - sa - viv, gil l'- ye - led rach. Cha - nu - kah, Cha - nu - kah,
L'- vi - vot, suf - ga - ni - yot b'- chol ba - yit yeish. Cha - nu - kah, Cha - nu - kah,

s'- vi - von sov sov, sov sov sov, sov sov sov, mah na - im va - tov.
chag na - im m'- od. Shi - ru na, zam - ru na, u - tz'- u lir - kod.

SINGABLE ENGLISH:
Chanukah, Chanukah, what a holiday.
Chanukah, Chanukah, time to sing & play.
Chanukah, Chanukah, watch the dreidl turn
Turn turn turn, turn turn turn,
    as the candles burn.

Chanukah, Chanukah, windows glowing bright.
Chanukah, Chanukah, latkes every night.
Chanukah, Chanukah, holiday of joy.
Dance & sing, spirit bring,
    every girl & boy.

חֲנֻכָּה, חֲנֻכָּה, חַג יָפֶה כָּל כָּךְ.
אוֹר חָבִיב מִסָּבִיב, גִּיל לְיֶלֶד רַךְ.
חֲנֻכָּה, חֲנֻכָּה, סְבִיבוֹן סֹב סֹב,
סֹב סֹב סֹב, סֹב סֹב סֹב, מַה נָעִים וָטוֹב.

חֲנֻכָּה, חֲנֻכָּה, אֵין חַלּוֹן בְּלִי אֵשׁ.
לְבִיבוֹת, סֻפְגָּנִיּוֹת, בְּכָל בַּיִת יֵשׁ.
חֲנֻכָּה, חֲנֻכָּה, חַג חָבִיב מְאֹד.
שִׁירוּ נָא, זַמְּרוּ נָא, וּצְאוּ לִרְקֹד.

Chanukah (Chag Yafeh)

Words: L. Kipnis
Music: Folktune, arr. Bonia Shur (ASCAP)

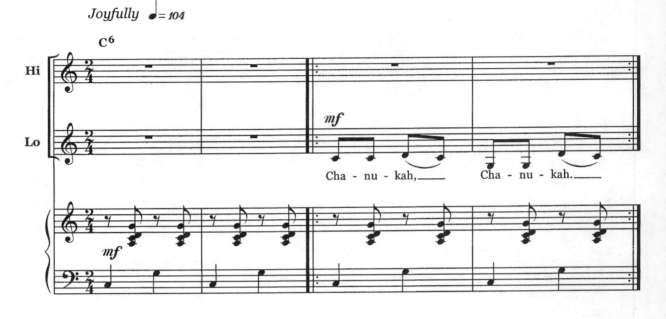

45

46

Chanukah is such a merry holiday.
Candles burn, a joy for every child.
Dreidl, spin spin spin.
How good and pleasant it is.

חֲנֻכָּה, חֲנֻכָּה, חַג יָפֶה כָּל כָּךְ.
אוֹר חָבִיב מִסָּבִיב גִּיל לְיֶלֶד רַךְ.
חֲנֻכָּה, חֲנֻכָּה, סְבִיבוֹן, סֹב סֹב,
סֹב סֹב סֹב, סֹב סֹב סֹב, מַה נָּעִים וָטוֹב.

Chanukah, no window is without
a flame. In every house there
are latkes and jelly doughnuts.
Let's go out to sing and dance.

חֲנֻכָּה, חֲנֻכָּה, אֵין חַלּוֹן בְּלִי אֵשׁ.
לְבִיבוֹת, סֻפְגָּנִיּוֹת, בְּכָל בַּיִת יֵשׁ.
חֲנֻכָּה, חֲנֻכָּה, חַג חָבִיב מְאֹד.
שִׁירוּ נָא, זַמְּרוּ נָא, וּצְאוּ לִרְקֹד.

47

Chanukah – A Noble Celebration
(This is Chanukah)

Jonathan & Aveeya Dinkin

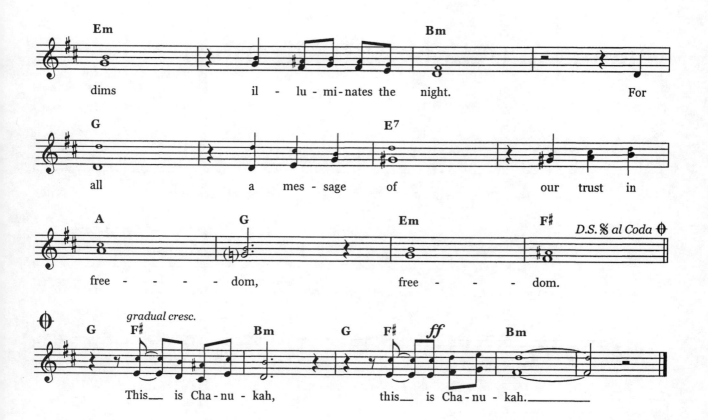

dims   il - lu - mi - nates the   night.   For

all   a   mes - sage   of   our   trust   in

free - - - dom,   free - - - dom.

This___ is Cha - nu - kah,   this___ is Cha - nu - kah._____

49

Chanukah (A Song of Dedication)

Words: Dan & Elysha Nichols
Music: Dan Nichols

com - fort the weak   when they're o-ver-whelmed with pain,___   to   hon-or___ the dreams of our

chil - dren young and old,___   and   to   be - come   the sto-ries that have   yet   to be told.___

Cha-nu - kah,   Cha-nu - kah,_____   as   we   fill   our   home with___ light.___   Cha-nu-

kah,   Cha-nu - kah,_____   we   ded - i - cate our - selves   to - night.   Cha-nu-

kah,   Cha-nu - kah,_____   great   mir-a - cles   bring   us___ here.___   Cha-nu-

kah,   Cha-nu - kah,_____   may   peace and love and bles - sing___ be   near.   May

peace and love and bles-sing___ be   near.   May   peace and love and bles-sing___ be   near.

Chanukah Catch

(3-part round)

Stephen Richards

I. Can-dles burn-ing all_ night_ long,_ Cha - nu-kah, oh, Cha - nu-kah._

II. Ju-dah, Ju-dah Mac - ca-bee_ fought the Greeks_ to_ make us free._ Me-

III. no, me-no, me - no, no - rah! Cha - nu, cha - nu, cha - nu-ki - ah!_

Chanukah - Festival of Lights

(4-part round)

Sara Krohn

I. Cha - nu - kah, fes - ti - val of lights.

II. Cel - e - brate the next eight nights.

III. We re - mem - ber Ju - dah Mac - ca - bee,

IV. and his strength that kept our peo - ple free.

Both songs also published in *The Complete Book of Jewish Rounds* (993194).

52

Chanukah Has Eight Nights
(3-part round)

Words: Cathi Turow
Music: Stephen Lawrence

Sing through once in unison, then start from beginning as a round.

Chanukah is Here

Jon Nelson

get lots of pres-ents and we feel so fine. We light the me-no-rah and it's

real-ly great___ to be with our fam-i-lies and cel-e-brate!___

Vs 3 I just can't wait for that ex-cit-ing time___ when we

o-pen up our pres-ents: "That one's yours, this one's mine!" The can-dles give off that

spe-cial glow___ that makes us feel co-zy and warm, you know!___

Br Yeah, that's Cha-nu-kah! Yeah, that's Cha-nu-kah!
Lat-kes!___ Drei-dles!___ Me-

Yeah, that's Cha-nu-kah too!
no-rahs!___ and that's what we want to do,___ ooh!___

we'll spread some Cha-nu-kah cheer.___ Our

fam-i-ly will all be near.___ Cha-nu-kah is___ here!___

Chanukah Lights

Words: Jeff Klepper & Dan Freelander
Music: Jeff Klepper

(instrumental)

1. On Cha - nu - kah___ we ded - i - cate___ with
2. To bring us all___ to - geth - er spe - cial
3. *Cha - nu - ki - ah___ re - minds us of the*

1. can - dles bring - ing light, the joy of friends and
2. bles - sings we re - cite,___ but the great - est gift of
3. *Tem - ple long a - go. A bright - ly burn - ing*

1. fam - i - ly___ in - creas - ing___ ev' - ry night!_____
2. Cha - nu - kah___ is my *cha - nu - ki - ah* light!_____
3. *neir ta - mid___ with can - dles___ all a - glow._____*

Chanukah Lights

Laurie Sucher

Verse 2:
Remember our heroes, the Maccabees
And the others who have slipped away.
Though their names may be forgotten,
Their deeds are still shining,
    lighting our paths today.   **CHORUS**

Verse 3:
So many unsung heroes,
Heroes along the way.
And with all that we have, we will
    try to be like them
So those who come after may say: **CHORUS**

Chanukah/Solstice

(4-part round)

Linda Hirschhorn

Turn-ing, turn-ing, spir-its yearn-ing, reach-ing for the night.

Col-ors go-ing, shad-ows grow-ing, dark-en-ing the light._____

An-cient sto-ry told, re-newed with the cold.

Mys-ter-y of light burned__ in-to the__ night.

N.B. To facilitate readability, this canon has been been printed linearly.
The entries are marked with Roman numerals.

Also published in *The Complete Book of Jewish Rounds* (993194).

The Chanukah Song

Mark Bernstein

off the me - no - rah, watch can - dles burn. Let's all play drei - dl,

spin on our turn___ on Cha - - nu - - kah.___

I'm so hap - py to be here to - day with friends and fam - 'ly I

love.___ I'm so luck - y to be here to - day to

cel - e-brate Cha - nu - kah!

Last time: to Coda ⊕

Vs 2

We've wait - ed all year_____ to o - pen our gifts, in -

deed it's a spe - cial time._____ We break the chal - lah,

we draw the blinds, e - ven drink some wine.

friends and fam - 'ly I love._____ I'm so

luck - y to be here to - day to cel - e - brate

Cha - nu - kah!

The Chanukah Story

Ruth Etkin

Sha-mas, sha-mas, light each light, re-live our days of glo-ry.

Help us to re-call the mir-a-cle of the Cha-nu-kah sto-ry.

1st candle: Num-ber one is for Mat-ta-thi-as;_____ to his
2nd candle: Num-ber two, for Ju-dah Mac-ca-bee, Lead-er

peo-ple he was true. He told An-ti-
of Ju-de-a's band. He led his sol-diers to

o-chus, "I will al-ways be a Jew."
vic-to-ry and__ chased the en-e-my from the land.

3rd candle:
Number three for all the Maccabees,
The soldiers who did fight
The Greek and Syrian army.
They fought with all their might.

4th candle:
Number four is for Yehudit.
As brave as brave could be,
She slew Holofemes
And earned her place in history.

5th candle:
Number five for the *chanukiyah*;
It's such a lovely sight.
Reminding us of Chanukah,
This *menorah* shines so bright.

6th candle:
Number six is for the holy oil
Burning brightly for eight days.
On Chanukah we give thanks to God
And sing God songs of praise.

7th candle:
Number seven is for the dreidl;
Twirl it, make it spin.
Watch the letters go 'round and 'round,
A *nun, gimel, hey,* and *shin.*

8th candle:
Number eight is for the miracle
Performed so long ago.
Each Chanukah we tell the tale
So everyone will know.

Come See the Candles

(2-part round)

Carol Boyd Leon

Drei Zich, Dreidele
(Turn Around, Little Dreidl)

Words: Chane Mlotek
(**English:** Rachel Buchman)
Music: Avrom Goldfaden

Joyfully ♩. = 62

Drei zich un, drei zich un, drei zich, shoin, drei-de-le.
Turn a-round, turn a-round. Spin, lit-tle drei-de-le.

Tants in a rin-ge-le, tants in a rei-ge-le. Eints, tsei, drai, eints, tsei, drai,
Turn a-round, turn a-round. Spin, lit-tle drei-de-le. 1, 2, 3, 1, 2, 3.

Repeat as desired, at various tempi

yin-ge-le, mei-de-le. Es iz shoin Cha-nu-ke do, shoin do!
Win, lit-tle drei-de-le. Cha-nu-kah's here___ to-night, to-night!

Eight Nights

Chuck Mitchell

Festival of Freedom

(5-part round)

Ronna Honigman

Also published in *The Complete Book of Jewish Rounds* (993194).

HaNeirot Halalu

(For 3 voices)

Words: Chanukah liturgy
Music: Judy Caplan Ginsburgh

These candles do we light.

הַנֵּרוֹת הַלָּלוּ אָנוּ מַדְלִיקִין.

Happy Chanukah

Larry Kaplan

We'll re-call the sto - ry of an - oth - er place and

time____ of the Mac - ca - bees,____ the Tem - ple, and a

drop of oil that shined and shined and

I.

shined. Hap - py Cha - nu - kah. It shined and shined.

II.

La la la la la la la la la la la la.

Hear Judea's Mountains Ringing

Words: Rufus Learsi
Music: A.W. Binder

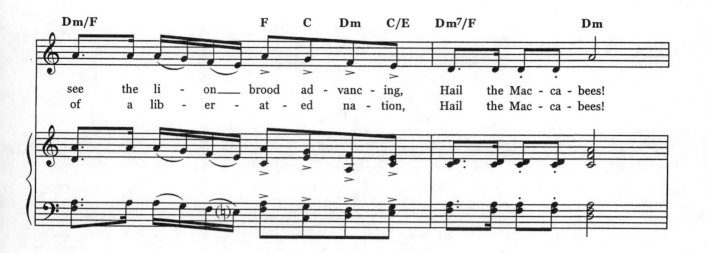

see the li - on___ brood ad - vanc - ing, Hail the Mac - ca - bees!
of a lib - er - at - ed na - tion, Hail the Mac - ca - bees!

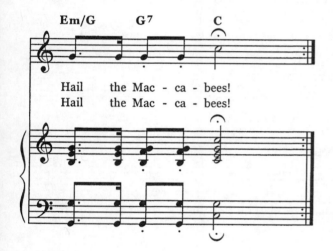

Hail the Mac - ca - bees!
Hail the Mac - ca - bees!

He's Brave!

Bernard Walters

Hinei Ba

G.F. Handel, from his oratorio
Judas Macabeus

See the conquering hero comes.
Sound the trumpets, beat the drums.
Sports prepare the laurels bring.
Songs of triumph to him sing.

הִנֵּה בָּא בְּהוֹד תָּקְפוֹ.
בַּחֲצוֹצְרוֹת הוֹדוּ לוֹ.
שִׁירוּ, זַמְּרוּ כָּל פְּדוּיָו
שִׁירַת נִצָּחוֹן אֵלָיו.

I Have a Little Dreidl

S. E. Goldfarb & S. S. Grossman

I'm a Dreidl

Jackie Cytrynbaum

1. I'm a drei - dl, can't you see the
2. Do you know what I can say:
3. Who will spin the Cha - nu - kah drei - dl?

way my friend is turn - - ing me?
Nun or *gi* - *mel,* *shin* or *hei.*
Will it be a *yin* - *gl* or a *mei* - *dl**?

* *boy or girl*

Don't you think I look so grand, un -

til it's time for me to land. Ker -

plunk,_____ ker - plunk._____

In the Candles' Rays

Words: Elma Ehrlich Levinger
Music: A.W. Binder

El - e - a - zar, brave___ and___ strong; Mac - ca - bees a -

gainst___ the___ throng; Han - nah, straight as a can - dle's flame,

sons who glo - ri - fied their moth - er's name:

D.C. al Fine

It's Chanukah Time

Julie Silver

And I re - mem - ber ____ ev - ery De - cem - ber we tell the tale we know so well, and all the fam - i - ly gath - ers hap - pi - ly; I wish Cha - nu - kah was mine all year. ____ I wish Cha - nu - kah was mine all year. ____

Last time: to Coda

D.S. ℅ (Vs 3) al Coda

Joys of Chanukah

Ruth Etkin

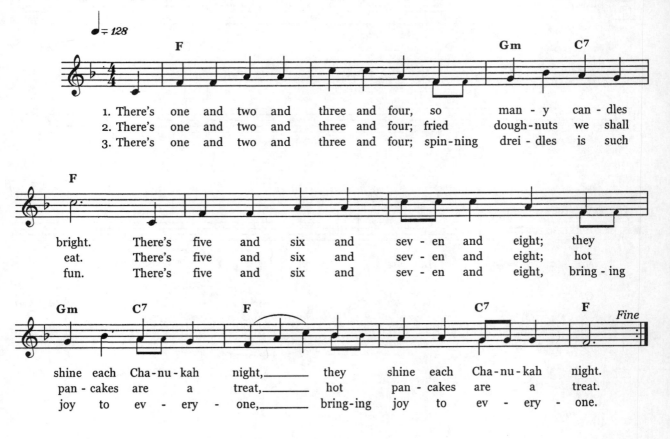

1. There's one and two and three and four, so man - y can - dles bright. There's five and six and sev - en and eight; they shine each Cha - nu - kah night,_____ they shine each Cha - nu - kah night.

2. There's one and two and three and four; fried dough-nuts we shall eat. There's five and six and sev - en and eight; hot pan - cakes are a treat,_____ hot pan - cakes are a treat.

3. There's one and two and three and four; spin-ning drei - dles is such fun. There's five and six and sev - en and eight, bring - ing joy to ev - ery - one,_____ bring-ing joy to ev - ery - one.

Judah Maccabee
(4-part round)

Ronna Honigman

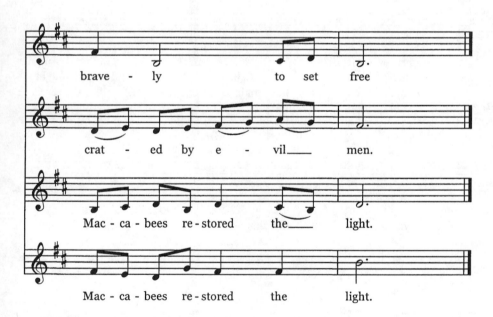

Also published in *The Complete Book of Jewish Rounds* (993194).

Judah Maccabee

Joe Black

one   called   Mac - ca - bee._____
beau - ty   they   re - stored._____
claimed   a   hol - i - day._____
Ju - dah   Mac - ca - bee._____

In   the win- dow____   shin - ing____ so____

bright,   I   can   see   the   Cha - nu - kah____

light.   And   it   gives   me   such_____   a

warm,   friend - ly   glow_____   when I   think   of   Ju - dah Mac-

ca - bee   so   long   a - go._____

Judah Maccabee

Robbie Solomon & Joel Sussman

1. Oh, when I was a boy,_____ my one and on - ly
2. Ah, my friends all thought me strange_____ and some-times would ex -
3. In the Po - lish un - der-ground,_____ I nev - er made a

joy was pre - tend - ing I was liv - ing in the past.
change a wor - ried look or word be - hind my back.
sound while run - ning through the for - est late at night.

So, to get my lit - tle thrills,_____ I'd storm down from the
No, they could - n't un - der - stand_____ the Ro - mans were at
Just like Mat - ta - thi - as' sons,_____ I knew the time would

hills, a wood - en sword held tight - ly in my grasp.
hand and they were get - ting read - y to at - tack.
come when I would need my cour - age to sur - vive.

Oh, Ju - dah Mac - ca - bee, how was I__ to see what you would mean to

me?_____ No { Sy - ri - an__ de - cree
Ro - man cav - al - ry
Ger - man in - fan - try } could make you bend__ your

knee, not Ju – dah Mac – ca – – bee.

bee.____ Get down, Ju – dah,____ get down, Ju – dah,____

____ get down, Ju – dah, get down, Ju – dah.____ Oh, Ju – dah Mac – ca –

bee, how was I___ to see what you would mean to me.____

No Ger – man in – fan – try could make you bend___ your knee, not Ju – dah Mac – ca –

bee, not Ju – dah Mac – ca – bee, not Ju – dah Mac – ca – – bee!

The Latke Song

Debbie Friedman

Let's Light the Chanukah Candles

(2-part round)

Bonia Shur (ASCAP)

Also published in *The Complete Book of Jewish Rounds* (993194).

Light One Candle

Peter Yarrow

Don't let the light go out,___ it's last-ed for so man-y years. Don't let the light go out,___ let it shine through our love and our tears.___

Light one can-dle for the strength that we need___ to nev-er be-come our own foe. Light one can-dle for those who are suf - fering the pain we learned___ so long a - go.

Light one can - dle for all we be - lieve___ in; let an - ger not tear us a - part. Light one can - dle to bind us to-geth - er with peace as the song in our heart.___

94

Vs 3

G
What is the mem - ory that's val - ued so high - ly that

Em   C
we keep a - live in that flame?   What's the com - mit- ment to

B7
those who have died___ when we cry out, "They've not died in vain"?

Em
We have come this___ far   al - ways be - liev - ing that

C   A   G   Em
jus - tice will some - how pre - vail.   This is the bur - den and

G   Em   C   D   G   B7 D.S. %al Coda
this is the prom - ise, and this is why we will not fail!___

E   Am   D   G   B7
Don't let the light go out,___ it's last - ed for so man - y years.

E   Am   D   G   B7
Don't let the light go out,___ let it shine through our love and our tears.___

E   Am   E   Am
Don't let the light go out.___   Don't let the light go out!

95

Light the Legend

Words: Susan Nurenberg
Music: Michael Isaacson

Light the Lights of Chanukah

Peter & Ellen Allard

2. Light the lights of Chanukah, second night. *(2x)*
   So special, so bright,
   So lovely on this Chanukah night.

   etc.

Light These Lights
(O Hear My Prayer)

Debbie Friedman

Lighting Candles in the Dark

Ros Schwartz

Peacefully ♩ = 96

Vs

1. First night of Cha-nu-kah,___ light one can-dle in the dark.___
2. Se-cond night of Cha-nu-kah,___ day-light fades___ so fast.___

Watch the flame grow strong and stead-y from this ti-ny spark.___
From these can-dles of to-day I wan-der to the past:___

From si-lence we___ weave songs___ with bles-sings and___ de-light.
One me-no-rah from___ my par-ents, one is mine___ a-lone,

We fill our hearts with joy___ and we fill___ our souls with light.___
two of clay by chil-dren fash-ioned, one___ more on its own.___

End

Hold on___ to the world of won-der in the dark-est night,___ then

Cha-nu-kah___ will nev-er end___ and you___ will shine___ with light.

3. Third night of Chanukah, the darkness drifts away
   As we light these five menorahs, we weave night into day.
   Hear our words of awe and wonder, blessings in God's name,
   See the glow of hope and promise in the steady flame.

4. Fourth night of Chanukah, watch the brightness grow.
   Breathe the beauty deep inside you as the candles glow.
   Some days you give your strength to me, some days I give you mine,
   For even in the darkest moments still the candles shine.

5. Candles five and six and seven, bind us to the light.
   Cast aside the growing shadows, let your soul shine bright,
   For the darkness has no power when we learn not to fear.
   Then light flows into every corner and God is with us here.

6. Eighth night of Chanukah, now my joy is tinged with pain,
   For even as I light these lights I know the dark will come again.
   Hold on to the world of wonder in the darkest night,
   Then Chanuka will never end ... and you will shine with light.

The Lights of Chanukah

Ray M. Cook

Little Dreidl

Ruth Etkin

1. Lit - tle drei - dl, spin spin spin. Lit - tle drei - dl, let's be - gin. Lit - tle drei - dl, who will win with a nun and a gi - mel and a hei and a shin?

2. Lit - tle drei - dl, let's have fun. Lit - tle drei - dl, we've be - gun. Lit - tle drei - dl, we have won. Neis ga - dol ha - yah sham.

Lots of Latkes
(3-part round)

English folk song, arr. Alan Leider

Also published in *The Complete Book of Jewish Rounds* (993194).

Ma-oz Tzur - Rock of Ages

Words: Mordechai (12-13th c.), **English:** G. Gottheil
Music: Trad., arr. A.W. Binder

N.B. Keyboard harmony differs somewhat from the guitar chords. Care should be taken if the two are used simultaneously.

Az eg - mor b' - shir miz - mor, cha - nu - kat ha - miz - bei - ach.
B'nei vi - nah y' - mei sh'mo - nah kav - u shir u - r' - no - nim.
And Your word___ broke their sword when our own strength failed___ us.
which will see all peo - ple free, ty - rants dis - ap - pear - ing.

Az eg - mor b' - shir miz - mor, cha - nu - kat ha - miz - bei - ach.
B'nei vi - nah y' - mei sh'mo - nah kav - u shir u - r' - no - nim.
And Your word___ broke their sword when our own strength failed___ us.
which will see all peo - ple free, ty - rants dis - ap - pear - ing.

מָעוֹז צוּר יְשׁוּעָתִי, לְךָ נָאֶה לְשַׁבֵּחַ;
תִּכּוֹן בֵּית תְּפִלָּתִי, וְשָׁם תּוֹדָה נְזַבֵּחַ.
לְעֵת תָּכִין מַטְבֵּחַ, מִצָּר הַמְנַבֵּחַ,
אָז אֶגְמֹ"ר, בְּשִׁיר מִזְמוֹר, חֲנֻכַּת הַמִּזְבֵּחַ.

יְוָנִים נִקְבְּצוּ עָלַי אֲזַי בִּימֵי חַשְׁמַנִּים,
וּפָרְצוּ חוֹמוֹת מִגְדָּלַי וְטִמְּאוּ כָּל הַשְּׁמָנִים.
וּמִנּוֹתַר קַנְקַנִּים נַעֲשָׂה נֵס לְשׁוֹשַׁנִּים,
בְּנֵי בִינָה יְמֵי שְׁמוֹ"נָה קָבְעוּ שִׁיר וּרְנָנִים.

107

Ma-oz Tzur

Words: Mordechai (12-13th c.)
Music: Max Janowski

Rock of Ages, let our song
     praise Your saving power.
You, amid the raging foes,
     were our sheltering tower.
Furious, they assailed us,
     but Your arm availed us,
And Your word broke their sword
     when our own strength failed us.

מָעוֹז צוּר יְשׁוּעָתִי, לְךָ נָאֶה לְשַׁבֵּחַ;
תִּכּוֹן בֵּית תְּפִלָּתִי, וְשָׁם תּוֹדָה נְזַבֵּחַ.
לְעֵת תָּכִין מַטְבֵּחַ, מִצָּר הַמְנַבֵּחַ,
אָז אֶגְמָ"ר, בְּשִׁיר מִזְמוֹר, חֲנֻכַּת הַמִּזְבֵּחַ.

Ma-oz Tzur

Words: Mordechai (12-13th c.)
Music: Benedetto Marcello (1686-1739)

bei - ach mi -tzar___ ham' - na bei - ach, Az___ eg - mor b'-

shir miz - mor, cha - nu - kat ha - miz - bei - ach.

Rock of Ages, let our song
    praise Your saving power.
You, amid the raging foes,
    were our sheltering tower.
Furious, they assailed us,
    but Your arm availed us,
And Your word broke their sword
    when our own strength failed us.

מָעוֹז צוּר יְשׁוּעָתִי, לְךָ נָאֶה לְשַׁבֵּחַ;
תִּכּוֹן בֵּית תְּפִלָּתִי, וְשָׁם תּוֹדָה נְזַבֵּחַ.
לְעֵת תָּכִין מַטְבֵּחַ, מִצַּר הַמְנַבֵּחַ,
אָז אֶגְמ"ר, בְּשִׁיר מִזְמוֹר, חֲנֻכַּת הַמִּזְבֵּחַ.

111

The Marching Maccabees

Jackie Cytrynbaum

The Verse can be sung against "So Brave and Bold" (page 166)

Menorah

Laura Berkson

Vs 1&2

Em   Em   D   C⁶

1. In the win-dow of a home___ in a qui - et north - ern town___
2. In the days___ that___ fol - lowed, oth-er Jew-ish homes were marked.

Em

___ hung the draw - ing of a Cha - nu - kah me - no - rah glow-ing
___ and the shad - owed arm of hat - red forced the town to face the

B⁷   Em

bright.___ I - saac was ex - cit - ed, for the
times.___ The sus - pects slipped a - way each time be -

Em D   C⁶   Em

five year - old knew well___ in a few days he would kin - dle the
fore they could be caught.___ No___ wit-ness to the crim-i-nals but

114

hol-i-day's first light._____ On a chill No-vem-ber eve-ning, the
on-ly to their crimes._____ You_ might think this was Kris-tallnacht, in

peace-ful town was shat-tered._____ Play-ing
nine-teen thir-ty eight_____ Strik-ing

down-stairs with his friends, young I-saac nev-er knew,_____
ter-ror in the Jews of Aus-tri-a and Ger-man-y_____

_____ as the sting of hat-red blan-ket-ed his bed with ti-ny
_____ but this took place in the foot-hills of the Rock-y Moun-tain

Me - no - rah,_____ the wheel of time__ is turn - ing__

Here_____ the tales of cour - age_____ still are spok - en_____

Vs 4

The fire in__the win-dow does-n't need a flame to burn._____ The

spark of love in ev - 'ryheart grows strong-er by the hour._____ And

those who seek to fan the flames of big-ot-ry shall watch_____ as their

fires are__ con-sumed by those who know that__ love__ is__ power._____

Me - no - rah_____ the flames_____ are burn-ing_____ but the

win - dow_____ in my soul can - not be brok - en_____

Me - no - rah, _____ the wheel of time _____ is turn - ing. _____

Here the tales _____ of cour - age _____ still are spok - en. _____

The Menorah

Connie Bryson

Mi Y'maleil? - Who Can Retell?

Folktune, arr. Eric Werner,
English: Judith K. Eisenstein

מִי יְמַלֵּל גְּבוּרוֹת יִשְׂרָאֵל! אוֹתָן מִי יִמְנֶה?
הֵן בְּכָל דּוֹר יָקוּם הַגִּבּוֹר גּוֹאֵל הָעָם.

שְׁמַע! בַּיָּמִים הָהֵם בַּזְּמַן הַזֶּה
מַכַּבִּי מוֹשִׁיעַ וּפוֹדֶה.
וּבְיָמֵינוּ כָּל עַם יִשְׂרָאֵל
יִתְאַחֵד, יָקוּם לְהִגָּאֵל!

Mi Zeh Hidlik

Words: L. Kipnis
Music: arr. Samuel Rosenbaum/J. M. Dunn

Playfully ♩. = 64

Mi zeh hid-lik nei-rot da-kim ka-ko-cha-vim ba-rom? Yod-im gam ti-no-kot ra-kim ki Cha-nu-kah ha-yom!

La, la, la, la, la, la, la, la, la, la, la, la, la, la, la, la, la, la, Cha-nu-kah ha-yom!

The candles shine brightly like the stars in the sky; everybody can tell that it is Chanukah.

מִי זֶה הִדְלִיק נֵרוֹת דַּקִּים
כַּכּוֹכָבִים בָּרוֹם?
יוֹדְעִים גַּם תִּינוֹקוֹת רַכִּים,
כִּי חֲנֻכָּה הַיּוֹם, כִּי חֲנֻכָּה הַיּוֹם!

127

Mi Zeh Hidlik

Hebrew lyrics: L. Kipnis
Music & English: Marshall A. Portnoy

מִי זֶה הִדְלִיק נֵרוֹת דַקִים
כַּכּוֹכָבִים בָּרוֹם?
יוֹדְעִים גַם תִּינוֹקוֹת רַכִּים,
כִּי חֲנֻכָּה הַיּוֹם, כִּי חֲנֻכָּה הַיּוֹם!

More Than Enough (The Chanukah Song)

Words: Doug Thiele
Music: Michael Isaacson (ASCAP)

130

My Candles (In the Window)

Words: Judith K. Eisenstein
Music: Chassidic

Neir Li (I Have a Candle)

Bonia Shur (ASCAP)

I have a thin little candle.
On Chanukah I will light my candle.
On Chanukah I will sing songs.

נֵר לִי דָקִיק, בַּחֲנֻכָּה נֵרִי אַדְלִיק.
בַּחֲנֻכָּה נֵרִי יָאִיר, בַּחֲנֻכָּה שִׁירִים אַשִׁיר:
לַ לַ ... נֵר לִי דָקִיק.

Never Give Up

Joel Sussman

Vs 3

D   **Bm⁷**

There was no way they___ were___ gon - na find___ a

Em   **A**   **F♯m⁷**

jar that was - n't smashed.___ There could be no flask___ that was

Bm⁷   **Em⁷**   **A⁷**

still in - tact___ there a - mong the smoke___ and___ ash.___ Then a

D   **Em**

guy an - nounced___ that he found___ an ounce___ of that prec - ious lan - tern oil,___

Bm   **G**   **D/F♯**   **Em⁷**   **A⁷**   **D**   **G**   **D**   *D.S. 𝄋 al Fine*

___ for you see, he nev - er gave up.___

144

Not By Might - Not By Power

Debbie Friedman,
based on Zechariah 4:6

O Chanukah, O Chanukah
(Oi Chanuke, Oi Chanuke)

Words: M. Rivesman (**English:** E. Guthmann)
Music: Chassidic, arr. A. W. Binder

while we   are   sing-ing, } the   can - dles are burn - ing___ low.
while we   are   play-ing,

shvin-der,   tsindt   kin - der.   Di   Di - nin-ke lich - te-lech ohn.

One   for each night, they___   shed a sweet light to re - mind us of days long a - go.

Zogt "Al ha - ni - sim", loybt Got far di   ni - sim, un kumt gi-cher tan - tsn in kon.

One   for each night, they___   shed a sweet light to re - mind us of days long a - go.

Zogt "Al ha - ni - sim", loybt Got far di   ni - sim, un kumt gi-cher tan - tsn in kon.

O, Ir Kleine Lichtelech

Words: Morris Rosenfeld
Music: Yiddish folksong, arr. J. Mark Dunn

accompaniment may be played an octave higher if desired

Eb   Cm   Fm   G   Cm

mu - ti - kait,   vun - der fun   a - mol,
zigt   a - mol."   Got,   dos gloibt   zich   koim,
hant   ge - hat.   Och   vi   tif   dos   rirt,

Fm   G   Cm

vun - der fun   a - mol.
Got,   dos gloibt   zich   koim.
Och   vi   tif   dos   rirt.

O you little candles, you are telling fairy tales,
Numberless stories,
You tell of bloodshed, brotherhood, and valor,
Wonders from long ago.

As I see you shimmering, a dream appears glimmering,
An old dream speaks:
"Jew, once you fought battles. Jew, once you were victorious."
God, it is so hard to believe.

Once you were a whole people, once you were a nation.
You yourself governed.
You owned your own land, you had a strong arm.
O how deeply it moves.
(tr. Joel N. Eglash)

Ocho Kandelikas

Flory Jagoda

Beautiful Chanukah is here. Eight candles for me.

One candle, two candles, ... eight candles for me.

Many parties I will have with happiness and pleasure.

The little pastries I will eat filled with almonds and honey.
(Original language: Ladino)

Oh, If I Were a Dreidl

Words: Judy Caplan Ginsburgh
Music: American folktune

♩ = 100

F　　　　　　　　　　　　　　　　　　　　　　**C**

1. Oh, if I were a drei-dl, I tell you what I'd do: I'd
2. Oh, if I were a lat-ke, I tell you what I'd do: I'd
3. Oh, if I were a can-dle, I tell you what I'd do: I'd
4. Oh, if I were some gelt,＿＿ I tell you what I'd do: I'd

F　　　　　　　　　　　　　　　　　　　　　**B♭**　　**F**

spin a-round a mil-lion times so I could play with you. If
fry my-self in lots of oil so I'd be food for you. If
jump in your me-no-rah,＿＿ so I'd be lit by you. If
find my way＿＿ to your house so I'd be a gift for you. If

B♭　　　　　　　　　　　　　　　**F**

I were a drei-dl, if I were a drei-dl, if
I were a lat-ke, if I were a lat-ke, if
I were a can-dle, if I were a can-dle, if
I were some gelt,＿＿ if I were some gelt,＿＿ if

B♭　　　　　　　　　　　**F**　　**C**　　**F**

I were a drei-dl, I'd spin a-round for you!
I were a lat-ke, oh, I'd be food for you!
I were a can-dle, oh, I'd be lit by you!
I were some gelt,＿＿ oh, I'd be a gift for you!

151

On Chanukah

Bernard Walters

On Happy Chanukah

Ray M. Cook

stand   up   tall   and   march   a - round   the   room!
dance   and   dance   and   melt   down__ to   the   ground!
turn - ing   'round   un - til   we__ fall. Ker-   plop!

On__ Cha - nu - kah, on__ Cha - nu - kah, on   hap - pyCha - nu - kah!   On__

Cha - nu - kah,   on__   Cha - nu - kah,   on   hap - py   Cha - nu - kah!

Once an Evil King

Words: H. Reinstein
Music: Harry Coopersmith

Also published in *The Complete Book of Jewish Rounds* (993194).

1-2-3-4-5 Brave Maccabees

Ray M. Cook

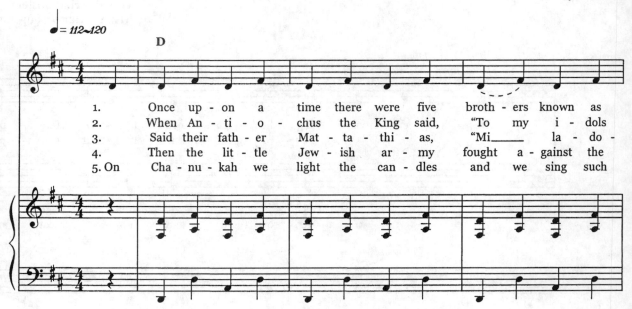

1. Once up-on a time there were five broth-ers known as
2. When An-ti-o-chus the King said, "To my i-dols
3. Said their fath-er Mat-ta-thi-as, "Mi_____ la-do-
4. Then the lit-tle Jew-ish ar-my fought a-gainst the
5. On Cha-nu-kah we light the can-dles and we sing such

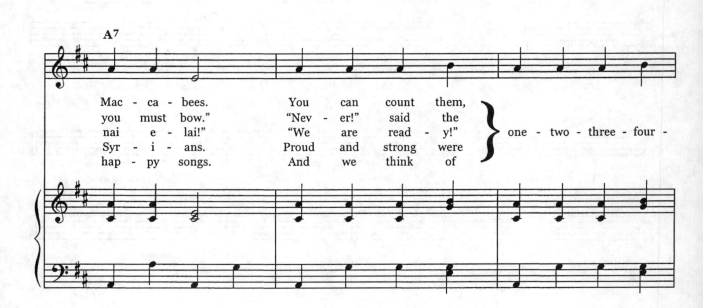

Mac - ca - bees. You can count them,
you must bow." "Nev - er!" said the
nai e - lai!" "We are read - y!" } one - two - three - four -
Syr - i - ans. Proud and strong were
hap - py songs. And we think of

five brave Mac - ca - bees, a - bees!

You can count them,
"Nev - er!" said the
"We are read - y!"
Proud and strong were
And we think of

one - two - three - four - five brave Mac - ca - bees, a - bees!

The Potato Song

Karen Daniel

Rise on Tiptoes

Words: Leo E. Turitz
Music: E. Zunser, arr. A.W. Binder

Rock of Ages

Words: M. Jastrow & G. Gottheil (translated from orig. Hebrew by Mordechai (12-13th c.))
Music: Ruth Bennett & Lisa Levine

Shehecheyanu

Craig Taubman

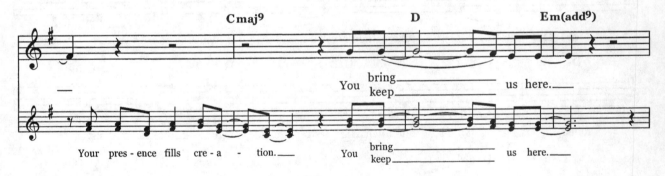

Shemen Zach

Words: Jacob Fichman
Music: Chaim Parchi, arr. J. M. Dunn

1. She-men zach hi-sag-ti li, v'-nei-rot chag hid-lak-ti li,
2. Ma-ka-bim li ka-mu az, ba-chu-rim li-bam no-az,

sod l'-nei-rot ei - leh. Or va-gil mam-ti-rim heim,
leiv mu-tzak mei-e - ven. mi-kol ir mi-kol miv-tzar,

neis ga-dol maz-ki-rim heim, neir l'-neir sa pe - leh!
heim geir-shu o-yeiv ach-zar, v'-hag'-u-lah hei-chei - lah!

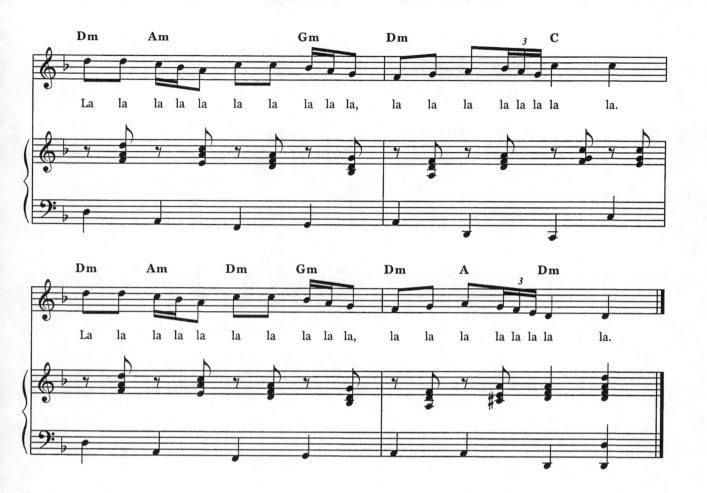

I found pure oil, and I lit the holiday candles.
There is a secret to these candles,
they sprinkle light and joy.

וְנֵרוֹת חַג הִדְלַקְתִּי לִי.
שֶׁמֶן זַךְ הִגַּתִּי,
סוֹד לַנֵּרוֹת אֵלֶּה.
אוֹר וְגִיל מַמְטִירִים הֵם,
נֵס גָּדוֹל מַזְכִּירִים הֵם,
נֵר לְנֵר שָׂא פֶּלֶא!

The Maccabees arose then, the hearts of men
were courageous--carved from stone.
From every city, from every fortress,
they repelled the cruel enemy,
and the redemption was launched.

מַכַּבִּים לִי קָמוּ אָז,
בַּחוּרִים לִבָּם נוֹעָז,
לֵב מוּצַק מֵאֶבֶן.
מִכָּל עִיר, מִכָּל מִבְצָר,
הֵם גֵּרְשׁוּ אוֹיֵב אַכְזָר,
וְהַגְּאֻלָּה הָאֵכֶלָה.

So Brave and Bold *

Fran Avni

Proudly ♩ = 100

Em

1. So brave___ and___ bold, the Mac - ca - bees re -
2. Re - sist - ed the might of e - vil___ men and___

Bm   Em

fused to___ bow down to___ their___ knees. } So brave___ and___ bold, the
cleansed the___ Tem - ple once___ a - gain.

Mac - ca - bees; we can hear them___ march - ing by.

This song can be sung against the Verse of "The Marching Maccabees" (page 112)

Sov, Sov S'vivon

Words: S. Bass
Music: P. Gruenspan

Joyfully ♩ = 120

Sov, sov, sov, sov, sov s'-vi-von mi-ru-sha-la-yim l'-Giv-on, l'-Giv-on. { Ba-ma-gal hi-ka-Eil, u-mi-sham l'-Yiz-r'-el. Sham k'-hal cha-lu-tzim b'-ma-chol ku-lam yotz-im. Sov, sov, s'-vi-von, ru-tzah u-tzah l'-Giv-on.

neis, v'-la-kol b'-kol hach-reiz: Hi-nei kam, ha-yah ha-neis, kol ha-a-retz k'-fa-deis, miB'-eir She-va v'-ad Dan, kol ha-a-retz haf-chah gan.

Spin, my top, around and around,
O spin past bush and pit and mound.
Past the vineyard, brook and rill,
Past valley and the hill.
On to Kishon, my dear,
When you meet a pioneer,
Greet him, bring him cheer:
"Miracles have happened here!"

סֹב, סֹב, סֹב, סֹב סְבִיבוֹן.
מִירוּשָׁלַיִם לְגִבְעוֹן.

מִגִּבְעוֹן סֹב עַד בֵּית אֵל, וּמִשָּׁם לְיִזְרְעֶאל.
שָׁם קְהַל חֲלוּצִים בְּמָחוֹל כֻּלָּם יוֹצְאִים.
סֹב, סֹב סְבִיבוֹן, רוּצָה אוּצָה לְגִבְעוֹן.

בַּמַּעְגָּל הִכָּנֵס וְלַכֹּל בְּקוֹל הַכְרֵז:
הִנֵּה קָם, הָיָה הַנֵּס, כָּל הָאָרֶץ כְּפַרְדֵּס,
מִבְּאֵר שֶׁבַע וְעַד דָּן, כָּל הָאָרֶץ הָפְכָה גַן.

Stop! Stop! Chanukah Top!

Words: Malcolm Stern
Music: Reuven Kosakoff

Sufganiyot

Joe Black

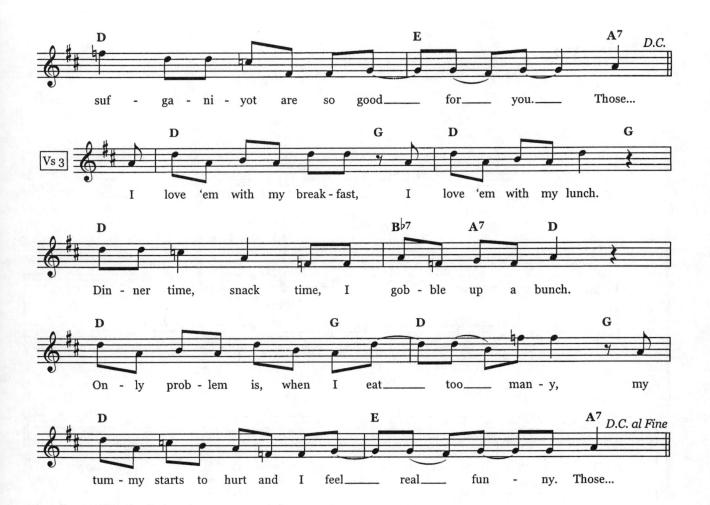

suf - ga - ni - yot are so good____ for____ you.____ Those...

Vs 3

I love 'em with my break - fast, I love 'em with my lunch.

Din - ner time, snack time, I gob - ble up a bunch.

On - ly prob - lem is, when I eat____ too____ man - y, my

tum - my starts to hurt and I feel____ real____ fun - ny. Those...

S'vivon

Words: M. Kipnis (**English:** S. Gewirtz)
Music: Wolli Kaelter

Twinkle, Twinkle, Little Light

Words: Stanley Brav
Music: Reuven Kosakoff

1. One light, two lights, three, then four, glow-ing, flam-ing more and more.
2. Mat - ta - thi - as, Si - mon, John, E - le - a - zar, Jon - a - than.

Five lights, six lights, sev-en and eight, thrill-ing sto - ries you re - late.
Ju - dah, brav - est of them all; saved the Tem - ple at God's call.

What Does Chanukah Mean to Me?

Ray M. Cook

1. Cha - nu - kah means lights,_____ stand - ing in a row,
2. Cha - nu - kah means free - dom, and the Mac - ca - bees,
3. Cha - nu - kah means glad - ness, Cha - nu - kah means fun,
4. Cha - nu - kah means wor - ship, grate - ful - ly we pray,

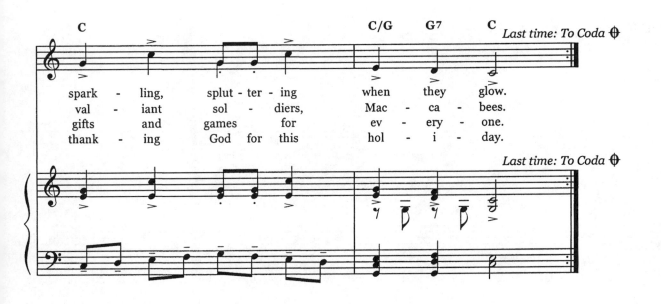

spark - ling,   splut - ter - ing   when   they   glow.
val - iant   sol - diers,   Mac - ca - bees.
gifts   and   games   for   ev - ery - one.
thank - ing   God   for   this   hol - i - day.

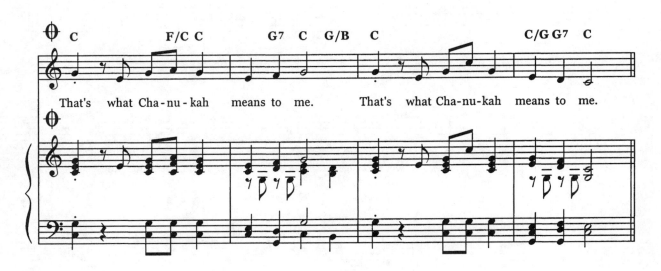

That's   what Cha - nu - kah   means to me.   That's   what Cha - nu - kah   means to me.

Where Is It?

Jackie Cytrynbaum

Tango ♩ = 112

Ch

| Cm | G | G7 |

I won - der where the oil_ is,____ I won - der where the

| Cm | G | Cm | G |

oil_ is,____ I won - der where the oil_ is,____ I

| G7 | Cm | *Fine* |

won - der where the oil_ could_ be.____

Lively

Vs

| C7 | F | C |

1. Look high as___ your nose, look low as___ your toes, look
2. Look in - side___ a box, look out - side with a fox, look
3. Look on top of a chair, look un - der now with care, look

| G | G7 | C | C7 | F |

high - er high - er high - er to the trees. Look low - er to your hips,__ look
in - side in - side in - side your__ shirt. Look out - side near a rock,__ look
on top on top on top of the land. Look un - der__ a ta - ble, look on

| C | G | G7 | *D.C. (Last time al Fine)* C |

high - er to your lips,__ look low - er low - er low - er to your knees.
in - side__ your sock,__ look out - side out - side out - side in the dirt.
top now that you're a - ble, look un - der un - der un - der-neath your hand.

With My Family (with Chanukah Verse)

Jeff Klepper & Dan Freelander

Y'mei HaChanukah

(For 2 voices, piano, & tambourine)

Chassidic, arr. Bonia Shur (ASCAP)

For a single-line version with chords see "O Chanukah O Chanukah."

bim._____ Al ha-ni-sim v'— al ha-nif-la-ot a—

bim,_____ ra-bim. Al ha-ni-sim, nif—la—ot

sher cho—l'—lu ha-Ma-ka—bim. Al ha-ni-sim v'—

cho—l'—lu ha-Ma—ka—bim, ha-Ma-ka-bim._____ Al ha-ni-sim v'—

O Chanukah, O Chanukah, come light the menorah.
Let's have a party, we'll all dance the hora.
Gather 'round the table, we'll give you a treat,
Shiny tops to play with and pancakes to eat.
And while we are playing, the candles are burning low.
One for each night, they shed a sweet light
To remind us of days long ago.

יְמֵי הַחֲנֻכָּה חֲנֻכַּת מִקְדָשֵׁנוּ
בְּגִיל וּבְשִׂמְחָה מְמַלְאִים אֶת לִבֵּנוּ
לַיְלָה וָיוֹם סְבִיבוֹנֵנוּ יִסֹב
סֻפְגָּנִיּוֹת נֹאכַל בָּם לָרֹב.
הָאִירוּ הַדְלִיקוּ נֵרוֹת חֲנֻכָּה רַבִּים.
עַל הַנִּסִּים וְעַל הַנִּפְלָאוֹת
אֲשֶׁר חוֹלְלוּ הַמַּכַּבִּים.

Yodlelay Do Potato

Peter & Ellen Allard

Other verse ideas:

I like to eat them with applesauce, I like to eat them all day …

I like to eat them with sour cream, I like to eat them all day …

I like to eat them in _____, I like to eat them all day …
(fill in a geographic location)

N.B. Both sections will work together.

Zoom, Zoom, Zoom

Connie Bryson

Zoom, zoom, zoom, hums the lit - tle drei - dl.

Zoom, zoom, zoom, Cha - nu - kah is here. Zoom, zoom, zoom,

Come and set the ta - ble. Zoom, zoom, zoom, hap - py time of year.

Spin the drei - dl, oh, what fun. Light the can - dles, one by one.

Count the days from one to eight. Ev - ery-bod - y, cel - e - brate!

N.B. Both sections will work together.

TITLE INDEX

TITLE INDEX

The Jewish Songster: Part I, 4th edition. Israel & Samuel Goldfarb, eds. Brooklyn: Religious Schools of Congregation Beth Israel Anshe Emes, 1925.

The Jewish Songster: Part II. Israel & Samuel Goldfarb, eds. Brooklyn: [Religious Schools of Congregation Beth Israel Anshe Emes], 1929.

Songs of Zion. Harry Coopersmith, ed. New York: Behrman House, Inc., 1942.

The Songs We Sing. Harry Coopersmith, ed. New York: The United Synagogue Commission on Jewish Education, 1950.

A Treasury of Jewish Folksong. Ruth Rubin, ed. New York: Schocken Books, Inc., 1950.

The Jewish Song Book, 3rd edition. Abraham Zevi Idelsohn, ed. Cincinnati: Publications for Judaism, 1951.

Binder, A.W. *Kabbalath Shabbath.* New York: Bloch Publishing Co., 1957.

Sabbath and Festival Songs for Young Singers. Samuel Rosenbaum, ed. New York: Mills Music, Inc., 1959.

Union Songster: Songs and Prayers for Jewish Youth. Eric Werner, ed. New York: CCAR Press, 1960.

Janowski, Max. *Chag Sameiach.* Chicago: Friends of Max Janowski, 1964. [catalogue no. 986420]

The New Jewish Song Book. Harry Coopersmith, ed. New York: Behrman House, Inc., 1965.

Barkan, Emanuel J. *Let us Sing!: Five Songs for Children.* Chicago: Friends of Jewish Music, 1966.

Shirey Yeladim: Songs for Children. Samuel Adler, mus. ed. New York: UAHC, 1970

More of the Songs We Sing. Harry Coopersmith, ed. New York: The United Synagogue Commission on Jewish Education, 1971.

Eisenstein, Judith Kaplan. *Heritage of Music: The Music of the Jewish People.* New York: UAHC, 1972.

Isaacson, Michael. *The Michael Isaacson Songbook: Vol. I.* New York: Transcontinental Music Publications, 2002. [catalogue no. 993192]

The Complete Jewish Songbook for Children: Manginot. Stephen Richards, ed. New York: Transcontinental Music Publications, 1992, 2002. [catalogue no. 991700]

The Complete Book of Jewish Rounds. J. Mark Dunn, ed. New York: Transcontinental Music Publications, 2002. [catalogue no. 993194]

The Complete Jewish Songbook: Shireinu. Joel N. Eglash, ed. New York: Transcontinental Music Publications, 2002. [catalogue no. 993210]

Ruach 5761 & 5763 Songbook: New Jewish Tunes. Joel N. Eglash, ed. New York: Transcontinental Music Publications, 2003. [catalogue no. 993221]

OTHER CHANUKAH MUSIC RESOURCES
FROM TRANSCONTINENTAL MUSIC PUBLICATIONS

18 Chanukah Songs for the Young Pianist
Rubinstein, Eli, arr.
Piano, Optional Voice (book) - 991075

A Chanukah Dreidle
Isaacson, Michael
SATB, Percussion - 991394

Al Hanisim (For the Miracles)
Solomon, Robbie
2-part choir, Keyboard, Flute, Clarinet - 993175

Al Hanissim (For The Miracles)
Kawarsky, J.A.
SATB, Clarinet, Piano - 993149

Al Hanissim (Sing to God)
Jacobson, Joshua/Netsky, Hankus, arr.
SATB, Piano, Optional Clarinet - 991306

Aleih Neiri
Parchi, Chaim/Jacobson, Joshua, arr.
Solo (Med), SATB, Rehearsal Keyboard - 992015

Banu Choshech Legaresh
Eddleman, David, arr.
2 Part Choir, Keyboard - 992068

Biy'mey Mattiyahu
Janowski, Max
Soli, SATB, Piano (Organ) - 986402

Candle Blessings for Chanukah
Jacobson, Joshua, arr.
Solo (med), SATB, Piano - 982044

Celebrate Chanukah
Phillips, Joel
SATB, Piano - 993106

Chanukah Candle Blessings/Maoz Tsur
Binder, A.W., arr./Jacobson, Joshua, ed.
Solo (Med), Rehearsal Piano - 992017

Chanukah Medley
Bronstein, Tamar
Small Instrumental Ensemble - 991258

Chanukah Song (Mi Y'maleil)
Chajes, Julius
Soli, SATB, Piano or Organ - 990211

Chanukah Variations
Jacobson, Joshua
SATB - 982003

Della Vita (Ma'oz Tsur)
Marcello, Benedetto/Jacobson, Joshua, arr.
Solo (High), Unison Choir, Cello, Keyboard - 982010

Drey Dreydeleh (Spin, Little Dreidel)
Jacobson, Joshua, arr.
SATB, Clarinet, Keyboard - 993199

Dreydl Variations (A New Spin On An Old Song)
Orr, Philip
SATB, Keyboard - 993212

Feast of Lights
Sargon, Simon, arr.
2 Part Choir, Keyboard - 991254

For All Your Miracles
Sargon, Simon
SATB, Keyboard - 991336

HaNeiros Halawlu (We Light the Menorah)
Lewandowski, Louis/Jacobson, Joshua, ed.
SA, Organ - 982069
SATB, Organ - 982001

Haneirot Halalu (Chanukah CD)
950003

Haneirot Halalu
Hemmel, Ronald
SATB, Piano - 993100

Hannukah Tarantella
Polansky, David/Jacobson, Joshua, arr.
2 Part Choir, Piano - 982083
SATB, Piano - 982035

Hanukah Lich'telech
Shur, Bonia, arr.
Solo (High), SAB, Keyboard - 984014

Hanukkah Madrigal (Mi Y'mallel)
Fromm, Herbert
Solo (High), SATB - 990239

I Have a Little Dreydel
Gelbart, Michael/Lazar, Matthew/Tayku, arr.
Solo (Med), SATB, Piano - 982002

In Honor of Hanukkah
Shur, Bonia, arr.
Solo (High), SSA, Piano - 984015

Light
Isaacson, Michael
SATB, Piano - 991023

Light the Legend
Isaacson, Michael
SATB, Keyboard - 991024
SSA, Keyboard - 992049
TTBB, Keyboard - 992050

OTHER CHANUKAH MUSIC RESOURCES
FROM TRANSCONTINENTAL MUSIC PUBLICATIONS

Ma'oz Tsur
Marcello, Benedetto/Jacobson, Joshua, ed.
Unison Choir - 982011

Maoz Tsur
Marcello, Benedetto/Zytowski, Carl, arr.
TTBB, Rehearsal Piano - 992055
SSA, Rehearsal Piano - 992056
Maoz Tsur/Mi Y'maleyl
Janowski, Max
Soli, SATB, Piano (Organ) - 986405

Maoz Tzur (Rock of Ages)
Roter, Bruce Craig/Levi, Michael, arr.
2-part choir, Keyboard - 993150

Ma'oz Tzur (Rock of Ages)
Adler, Samuel, arr.
SSA, Keyboard - 990314

Mi Yemalel (Who Can Retell?)
Helfman, Max
SATB, Rehearsal Piano - 991500

Mi Y'maleil
Barnett, Steve, arr.
SATB, Rehearsal Piano - 991294

Mi Y'maleil (Who Can Retell?)
Flummerfelt, Joseph, arr.
SATB, Rehearsal Piano - 993104

Mi Y'maleil? (Who Can Retell?)
Richards, Stephen, arr.
SATB, Brass Quartet, Keyboard - 992041
Vocal Score - 992064

Mi Zeh Hidlik
Barnett, Steve, arr.
SATB, Rehearsal Piano - 991295

Mi Zeh Y'maleil
Jacobson, Joshua, arr.
Solo, SATB, Drum, Rehearsal Piano - 992016

More Than Enough
Isaacson, Michael
Solo Voice, SATB, Piano - 993113

O Ir Kleyne Likhtelekh (O, You Little Candles)
Eddleman, David, arr.
2 Part Choir, Keyboard - 992069

O Mighty Hand (Dor Nifla)
Goldman, Maurice
SATB, Organ or Piano - 991033

Ocho Kandelikas (8 Candles)
Jagoda, Flory/Jacobson, Joshua, arr.
Solo (High), SATB, Guitar, Percussion - 982015
Solo (Med), SA, Guitar - 982070

Rock of Ages (Maoz Tsur)
Adler, Samuel, arr.
SATB, Keyboard - 990134

Shemen Zach (Pure Oil)
Parchi, Chaim/Jacobson, Joshua, arr.
Solo, SATB, Piano, Opt. Electric Guitar - 991340

Simu Shemen (Fill the Lanterns)
Eddleman, David, arr.
2 Part Choir, Keyboard - 992067

Sing a Song of Chanukah
Isaacson, Michael
SATB, Keyboard - 991389

S'vivon
Barnett, Steve, arr.
SATB, Rehearsal Piano - 991293

S'vivon
Flummerfelt, Joseph, arr.
SATB, Rehearsal Piano - 993105

S'vivon (The Top)
Helfman, Max, arr.
SATB - 991501

The Light From Long Ago
Sheldon, Gary/Bronshvag, Michael
Unison Children's Choir, Keyboard - 993168

Y'mei Chanukah
Barnett, Steve, arr.
SATB, Rehearsal Piano - 991292

**Zemer l'Shabbat Vachanukah
(A Song For The Sabbath Of Chanukah)**
Eisenstein, Judith Kaplan
SATB *a cappella*, Rehearsal Piano - 992079

---

www.TranscontinentalMusic.com